teacher's friend publications

December

a creative idea book
for the
elementary   teacher

written and illustrated
by
Karen Sevaly

Copyright © 1986
Teacher's Friend Publications
All rights reserved.
Printed in the United States of America.
Published by Teacher's Friend Publications
11521 Davis Street, Moreno Valley, CA 92387

ISBN-0-943263-03-4

TO TEACHERS AND CHILDREN EVERYWHERE.

Table of Contents

MAKING THE MOST OF IT! 7

    What is in this book 8
    How to use this book 8
    Adding the color 9
    Laminators 9
    Ditto masters 10
    Bulletin board backgrounds 11
    Lettering and headings 11

CALENDAR - DECEMBER 13

    December calendar and activities 14
    Calendar topper 17
    Blank calendar 18

HOLIDAY ACTIVITIES 19

    My letter to Santa! 20
    Holiday word find 21
    My Santa book 22
    Holiday trivia 23
    My shopping list! 26
    Snowman story 27
    Elf wheel 28
    Snowman math 30
    Dreaming of Christmas 31
    Santa color page 32

FOR GOODNESS SAKE! 33

    December awards 34
    Award ornaments 35
    Bookmarks 36
    Pencil toppers 37
    Awards 38
    Holiday carolers 40
    Holiday finger puppets 42

HOLIDAY CRAFTS 43

    Wreath and sleigh 44
    Snow scene and reindeer 45
    Stand up Santa 46
    Angel ornament 47
    Movable reindeer 48
    Movable Santa 49

Santa Claus puppet 50
Stained glass pictures 52
Christmas tree puppet 54
Reindeer antlers 55
Snowman card 56
Santa card 57
Christmas countdown 58

MERRY CHRISTMAS, MANY WAYS 59

International Christmas tree 60
Customs and Traditions 61
International greetings 64
"Peace on Earth" 65
Dove of peace 66

CHRISTMAS IN MEXICO 67

Feliz Navidad word find 69
International children - Mexico 70
Creative writing page 72

CHRISTMAS IN ITALY 73

"La Befana" 75
International children - Italy 76
Creative writing page 78

CHRISTMAS IN HOLLAND 79

Poems from Sinterklaas 81
International children - Holland 82
Wooden shoe 84
Windmill 85
Creative writing page 86

CHRISTMAS IN SWEDEN 87

Santa Lucia sweet rolls 89
International children - Sweden 90
Santa Lucia headwreaths 92

HANUKKAH 93

Hanukkah word find 95
International children - Israel 96
Star of David 98
Menorah 99
Dreydl 100

BULLETIN BOARDS AND MORE! 101

    December bulletin boards 102
    Stocking pattern 105
    Santa's list 106
    Partridge and pear tree 107
    Santa sign man 108
    French horn and angel 109

ANSWER KEY 111

Making the most of it!

Making the Most of It!

WHAT IS IN
THIS BOOK:

You will find the following in each monthly idea book from Teacher's Friend Publications:

1. A calendar listing every day of the month with a classroom idea.

2. At least four new student awards to be sent home to parents.

3. Three new bookmarks that can be used in your school library or given to students by you as "Super Student Awards."

4. Numerous bulletin board ideas and patterns pertaining to the particular month.

5. Easy to make craft ideas related to the monthly holidays.

6. Dozens of activities emphasizing not only the obvious holidays but also the often forgotten celebrations, such as; Hannukkah and Santa Lucia Day.

7. Crossword puzzles, word finds, creative writing pages, booklet covers, games and much more.

8. Scores of classroom management techniques, the newest and the best.

HOW TO USE
THIS BOOK:

Every page of this book may be duplicated for individual classroom use.

Some pages are meant to be used as duplicating masters and used as student work sheets. Other pages may be copied onto construction paper or used as they are.

If you have access to a print shop, you will find that many pages work well when printed on index paper. This type of paper takes crayons and felt markers well and is sturdy enough to last and last. (The bookmarks work particularly well on index paper.)

Lastly, some pages are meant to be enlarged with an overhead or opaque projector. When we say enlarge, we mean it! Think BIG! Three, four or even five feet is great! Try using colored butcher paper or poster board so you don't spend all your time coloring.

Making the Most of It!

ADDING THE
COLOR:

Putting the color to finished items can be a real bother to teachers in a rush. Try these ideas:

1. On small areas, water color markers work great. If your area is rather large, switch to crayons or even colored chalk or pastels.

    (Don't worry, lamination or a spray fixative will keep the color on the work and off of you. No laminator or fixative? That's okay, a little hair spray will do the trick.)

2. The quickest method of coloring large items is to simply start with colored paper. (Poster board, butcher paper or large construction paper work well.) Add a few dashes of a contrasting colored marker or crayon and you will have it made.

3. Try cutting character eyes, teeth, etc. from white typing paper and gluing them in place. These features will really stand out and make your bulletin boards come alive.

    For special effects add real buttons or lace. Metallic paper looks great on stars and belt buckles, too.

LAMINATORS:

If you have access to a roll laminator you already know how fortunate you are. They are priceless when it comes to saving time and money. Try these ideas:

1. You can laminate more than just classroom posters and construction paper. Try various kinds of fabric, wallpaper and gift wrapping. You'll be surprised at the great combinations you come up with.

    Laminated classified ads can be used to cut headings for current event bulletin boards. Colorful gingham fabric makes terrific cut letters or scalloped edging. You might even try burlap! Bright foil gift wrapping paper will add a festive feeling to any bulletin board.

    (You can even make professional looking bookmarks with laminated fabric or burlap. They are great holiday gift ideas!)

2. Felt markers and laminated paper or fabric can work as a team. Just make sure the markers you use are permanent and not water bases. Oops, make a mistake! That's okay. Put a little ditto fluid on a tissue, rub across the mark and presto, it's gone! (Dry transfer markers work great on lamination, too.

LAMINATORS:
(continued)

3. Laminating cut-out characters can be tricky. If you have enlarged an illustration onto poster board, simply laminate first and then cut it out with an art knife. (Just make sure the laminator is plenty hot.)

One problem may arise when you paste an illustration onto poster board and laminate the finished product. If your paste-up is not 100% complete, your illustration and posterboard may separate after laminating. To avoid this problem, paste your illustration onto poster board that measures slightly larger. This way, the lamination will help hold down your paste-up.

4. When pasting up your illustration always try to use either rubber cement, an artist's spray adhesive or a glue stick. White glue, tape or paste does not laminate well.

5. Have you ever laminated student made place mats, crayon shavings, tissue paper collages, or dried flowers? You'll be amazed at the variety of creative things that can be laminated and used in the classroom, or as take-home gifts.

DITTO MASTERS:

Many of the pages in this book can be made into masters for duplicating. Try some of these ideas for best results:

1. When using new masters, turn down the pressure on the duplicating machine. As the copies become light, increase the pressure. This will get longer wear out of both the master and the machine.

2. If the print from the back side of your original comes through the front when making a master or photocopy, slip a sheet of black construction paper behind the sheet. This will mask the unwanted black lines and create a much better copy.

3. Trying to squeeze one more run out of that worn master can be frustrating. Try lightly spraying the inked side of the master with hair spray. For some reason, this helps the master put out those few extra copies.

4. Several potential masters in this book contain instructions for the teacher. Simply cover the type with correction fluid or a small slip of paper before duplicating.

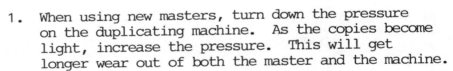

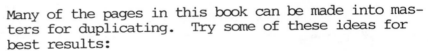

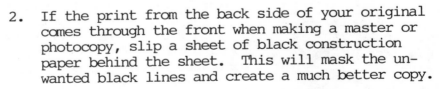

Making the Most of It!

BULLETIN BOARD
BACKGROUNDS:

Creating clever bulletin boards for your classroom need not take fantastic amounts of time and money. With a little preparation and know-how you can have different boards each month with very little effort. Try some of these ideas:

1. Background paper should be put up only once a year. Choose colors that can go with many themes and holidays. The black butcher paper background you used as a spooky display in October will have a special dramatic effect in December when you use letters cut from holiday foil gift wrap paper.

2. Butcher paper is not the only thing that can be used to cover the back of your board. You might like to try colored burlap. Just fold it up at the end of the year to reuse again.

   Wallpaper is another great background cover. Discontinued rolls can be purchased for next to nothing at discount hardware stores. Most can be wiped clean and will not fade like construction paper. (Do not glue wall paper directly to the board, just staple or pin in place.)

LETTERING AND
HEADINGS:

Not every school has a letter machine that produces perfect 2" or 4" letters from construction paper. (There is such a thing, you know.) The rest of us will just have to use the old stencil and scissor method. But wait, there is an easier way!

1. Don't cut individual letters. They are difficult to pin up straight, anyway. Instead, hand print bulletin board titles and headings onto strips of colored paper. When it is time for the board to come down, simply roll it up to use again next year.

   Use your imagination. Try cloud shapes and cartoon bubbles. They will all look great.

LETTERING AND
HEADINGS:
(continued)

2. Hand lettering is not that difficult, even if your printing is not up to penmanship standards. Print block letters with a felt marker. Draw big dots at the ends of each letter. This will hide any mistakes and add a charming touch to the overall effect.

SCHOOL TIME

If you are still afraid about free handing it, try this nifty idea: Cut a strip of poster board about 28" X 6". Down the center of the strip cut a window with an art knife measuring 20" X 2". There you have it, a perfect stencil for any lettering job. All you do is write your letters with a felt marker within the window slot. Don't worry about uniformity, just fill up the entire window heighth with your letters. Move your poster board strip along as you go. The letters will always remain straight and even because the poster board window is straight.

3. If you must cut individual letters, use this idea:

Cut numerous sheets of construction paper into $4\frac{1}{2}$" X 6" squares. (Laminate first if you can.) Cut letters as shown in the illustration. No need to measure, irregular letters will look creative not messy.

WELCOME BA[CK] TO SCHOOL!

A B C D
E F G H I J K
L M N O P Q R
S T U V W X Y Z

Calendar

December

December

(HANUKKAH is celebrated on the twenty-fifth day of the Hebrew month of Kislev.)

1   ROSA PARKS, a black seamstress, began the American civil rights movement by refusing to give up her seat on a Montgomery, Alabama bus. (Discuss with your class what changes came about by this and other events in the 1960s.

2   On this date in 1823, the MONROE DOCTRINE was declared by President James Monroe at his annual address to Congress. (Ask students to find out what this policy meant to the United States and Latin America.)

3   WILLIAM HERSCHEL, an English astronomer, discovered the planet Uranus on this day in 1781. (Ask students to locate Uranus on a map of the solar system.)

4   Mexico celebrates the DAY OF THE ARTISANS in honor of the country's laborers. (Ask students if they know which day Americans honor their laborers.)

5   WALT DISNEY, creator of Mickey Mouse, was born on this day in 1901. (Show the class one of Disney's nature films in celebration.)

6   Today is SINTERKLAAS DAY in the Netherlands. (Ask students to say Sinterklaas fast, ten times. The children will soon see how he came to be called "Santa Claus" in the United States.)

7   Today is the anniversary of the bombing of PEARL HARBOR by the Japanese in 1941. (Ask students to ask parents or grandparents where they were on that day.)

8   ELI WHITNEY, American inventor, was born on this day in 1765. (Ask students to find out what he invented and what it meant to the history of the United States.)

9   The famous American clown, EMMETT KELLY, was born on this day in 1898. (As an art project, students may wish to paint their own clown faces in celebration.

10   Today is UNITED NATIONS HUMAN RIGHTS DAY! (Ask students to list what they consider to be basic human rights.)

11 UNICEF was established on this day in 1946. (Instruct students to find out what this organization does and what the letters U.N.I.C.E.F. represent.)

12 INDEPENDENCE DAY in Kenya was declared on this day in 1963. (Ask students to research which country ruled Kenya before their freedom was declared.)

13 Today, in Sweden, people celebrate SANTA LUCIA'S DAY with a special candlelight parade. (Students may wish to make Santa Lucia headwreaths in celebration.)

14 The SOUTH POLE was discovered on this day in 1911 by the Norwegian explorer Roald Amundsen. (Ask students to research the event and trace his voyage on the classroom map.)

15 The BILL OF RIGHTS became a part of the United States Constitution on this day in 1791. (Read them aloud to your class. For a copy on full sized parchment paper, send 45 cents to the General Services Administration, Washington, D.C., 20408.)

16 On this day in 1773, American colonists dumped British tea in the Boston Harbor. This event was known as the BOSTON TEA PARTY. (Ask students to find out what the colonists were protesting.)

17 ORVILLE and WILBUR WRIGHT made the first successful airplane flight in 1903. The flight lasted only 12 seconds. (Students might like to see if paper airplanes can stay aloft as long.)

18 On this day in 1865, the 13th AMENDMENT to the U.S. Constitution was ratified. (Select a student to read it to the class and discuss its meaning.)

19 In 1958, President Eisenhower greeted the world on the first RADIO VOICE BROADCAST from space via satellite. (Explain the concept of satellite transmission to your class.)

20 In 1803, the United States purchased more than a million square miles of territory from France for $20 an acre. (Ask students to locate the territory known as the LOUISIANA PURCHASE on the classroom map.)

21 Today is FOREFATHER'S DAY in honor of our ancestors, the pilgrims, landing at Plymouth, Massachusetts in 1620. (Ask students to find out how many days they spent on their journey.)

December

22   Today is WINTER SOLSTICE, the shortest day of the year. (Ask students to locate the time of sunrise and sunset in the local newspaper.)

23   On this day in 1975, President Ford signed the METRIC CONVERSION ACT. (Ask students to measure their height using both standard and metric measurement.)

24   The Christmas song, "SILENT NIGHT" was composed and first sung on this day in 1818. (Find the story of this special night and read it to your class.)

25   Today is CHRISTMAS DAY! (Assign a country to each student and ask them to find out how their country celebrates this special day.)

26   Today is BOXING DAY in Great Britain, Canada, and some countries in Europe. (Ask students to find out how it is celebrated and why they call it "Boxing Day.")

27   The famous French chemist, LOUIS PASTEUR, was born on this day in 1822. (Ask students to research his discoveries.)

28   CHEWING GUM was first patented by William Semple on this day in 1869. (You may like to permit gum chewing in class for this one day in celebration.)

29   Today marks the anniversary of the WOUNDED KNEE MASSACRE. More than 200 native Americans were killed by U.S. soldiers on this day in 1890. (Ask students their thoughts about the struggles of the American Indians.)

30   Congress authorized the minting of a new HALF DOLLAR on this day in 1963. (Ask students whose portrait is displayed on this coin and why?)

31   Today is NEW YEAR'S EVE! (Ask students to list resolutions the world could make in order to better the life of all mankind.)

Calendar Topper

December

sun	mon	tue	wed	thu	fri	sat

Holiday Activities

My Letter to Santa!

_____
date

Dear Santa,

_____

_____

_____

_____

_____

_____

_____

_____

_____

_____

_____

_____

_____

_____

_____

_____

Signed _____

Holiday Word Find

UNSCRAMBLE SANTA'S REINDEER NAMES.   ACTIVITY 1

Z N E T I L B   _ _ _ _ _ _ _

P D I U C   _ _ _ _ _

X I N V E   _ _ _ _ _

H S R E A D   _ _ _ _ _ _

M O T E C   _ _ _ _ _

C A N D R E   _ _ _ _ _ _

D U L O H P R   _ _ _ _ _ _ _

C R N E A R P   _ _ _ _ _ _ _

D D N O R E   _ _ _ _ _ _

If you need help.... Dasher, Dancer, Prancer, Vixen, Comet, Cupid, Donder, Blitzen, and Rudolph!

ACTIVITY 2

CAN YOU FIND ALL OF THE DECORATIONS FOR THE TREE?

CANDYCANES, ORNAMENTS, ANGEL, TINSEL, STAR, BOWS, BELLS, GARLAND, ICICLES, LIGHTS and PINECONES

```
L K I J H O P L L L M N B V C S T A R H N J K O P
W C V G H J B O W S S D F G Y T R E D F V B N M K
S D R T G F H R Y N J H U I K D E R T I G T Y H J
G G T Y H J U N R E W Q R T Y U I K L C D R T Y U
A D E R T H C A N D Y C A N E S K L J I D F T F G
R F T Y J G H M N B Y N A L R U D R T C F G Y U M
L F G T H Y N E J K R E W X Z A N G E L M J G Y R
A D E R T Y H N D F B C F R T Y H J H E G H N M K
N F T F T G H T I N S E L B H J U I L S D R T S X
D F G T H Y U S K I L O J E F T G H U J N B V C X
P I N E C O N E S T Y H N L G Y U I P R E W D S F
B G H U Y T F G H J U I K L G V B N M K L P O I U
S E R T H J U I O K J M N S E D C V B N M K J U Y
S E R T G F V B H J K L I G H T S E W R T F G H J
A S D C V B N M K J H G F D S A T R E W Y U I O P
R F D E S W Q A Z X C V B H G Y T U I J K L O P U
```

MY SANTA BOOK

22

Holiday Trivia

To play Holiday Trivia, first enlarge this Christmas Tree gameboard onto posterboard or draw the tree on the class chalkboard. Next, divide the class into two teams, the RED team and the GREEN team.

To start the game, toss a coin to see which team will go first.

Each team has separate questions and answers. When a team lands on a numbered space, refer to the corresponding numbered question. If the team answers the question correctly, they may move to the next space. If the answer is incorrect, they must give up their turn.

The object of the game is to see which team can get to the top of the tree first.

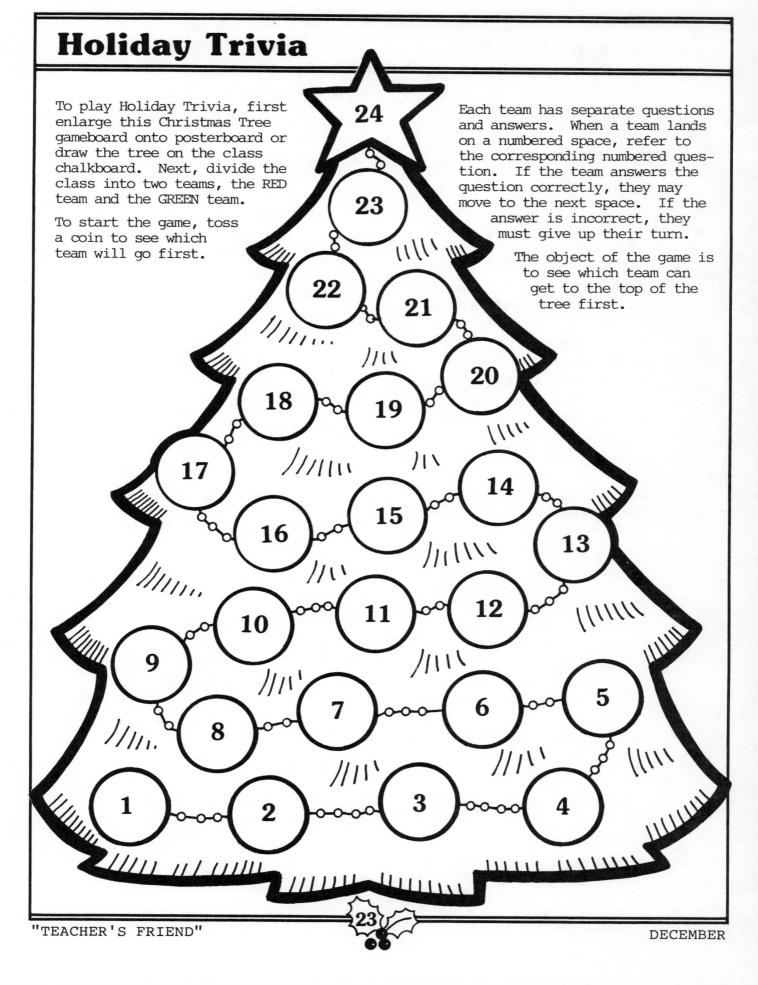

Holiday Trivia

1. What day is Christmas Day?

2. Name the red flower commonly used at Christmas.

3. Who were the Magi?

4. What is the name of the special candlestick used during Hanukkah?

5. Name three of Santa's reindeer.

6. What song contains the phrase "Fa-la-la-la-la-la-la-la-la?"

7. What is the name of the famous singing chipmunk?

8. What was Scrooge's favorite saying in "A Christmas Carol?"

9. Name two places Santa puts presents for children.

10. In what country would you wish someone "Joyeux Noel?"

11. What did Mary ride to the stable where she gave birth to Jesus?

12. What is a crèche?

13. In the song "The Twelve Days of Christmas," what was sent on the eighth day?

14. What is the Jewish holiday celebrated in December?

15. In one holiday song, a boy claims all he wants for Christmas are two things. What are they?

16. Name the famous Christmas ballet enjoyed by children.

17. What are latkes?

18. What are the two Christmas colors?

19. Where does Santa live?

20. In the Bible story about the first Christmas, why did Mary and Joseph go to Bethlehem?

1. What happens when you stand under mistletoe?

2. Who was chosen to guide Santa on Christmas Eve?

3. What do bad boys and girls get for Christmas?

4. What is Santa Claus called in England?

5. In what country would you wish someone "Feliz Navidad?"

6. Who's "nipping at your nose" when you go outside in winter?

7. What is the date of Christmas Eve?

8. What do Dutch children leave out for Santa to fill with presents?

9. Who are Santa's helpers?

10. How many turtle doves were sent in the song "The Twelve Days of Christmas?"

11. What famous snowman do we sing about at Christmas?

12. Name one of the three spirits who visited Scrooge on Christmas Eve?

13. In what country would you find a piñata on Christmas?

14. Name one ingredient in mince pie.

15. Name a food item people often string together to make garlands.

16. Who first saw the star of Bethlehem in the Bible story?

17. How many reindeer does Santa have?

18. Who is Kris Kringle?

19. When is the first day of winter?

20. In the song about "Rudolph," what is the weather like on Christmas Eve?

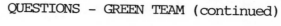

QUESTIONS - RED TEAM (continued)

21. What do people hang on their doors at Christmas?

22. What is said that animals do on Christmas Eve?

23. What is "roasting on an open fire" in "The Christmas song?"

24. Name three words Santa says when he's happy.

QUESTIONS - GREEN TEAM (continued)

21. Who is "coming to town" in the popular Christmas carol?

22. What is the "top" called that Jewish children play with?

23. What is the name of the little crippled boy in "A Christmas Carol?"

24. Name one of the gifts brought to Jesus by the Three Wise Men.

ANSWERS - RED TEAM

1. December 25
2. Poinsettia
3. The Three Wise Men
4. Menorah
5. Dasher, Dancer, Prancer, Vixen, Comet, Cupid, Donder, Blitzen and Rudolph
6. "Deck the Halls"
7. Alvin
8. "Bah, Humbug!"
9. Under the tree and inside stockings
10. France
11. Donkey
12. Replica of the stable where Jesus was born
13. Eight maids a-milking
14. Hanukkah
15. Two front teeth
16. "The Nutcracker"
17. Potato pancakes which are made during Hanukkah
18. Red and Green
19. The North Pole
20. They went to be counted and to pay taxes
21. Wreaths
22. They talk
23. Chestnuts
24. "Ho, ho, ho!"

ANSWERS - GREEN TEAM

1. You get kissed
2. Rudolph
3. Coal in their stockings
4. Father Christmas
5. Mexico or Spain
6. Jack Frost
7. December 24
8. Wooden Shoes
9. Elves
10. Two turtle doves
11. Frosty
12. The Ghost of Christmas Past, Present and Future
13. Mexico
14. Raisins, apples, cinnamon, cloves, nutmeg, sugar, and sometimes meats.
15. Popcorn and cranberries
16. The Three Wise Men
17. With Rudolph, nine
18. Santa Claus
19. December 22
20. Foggy
21. Santa Claus
22. Dreydl
23. Tiny Tim
24. Gold, Frankincense and Myrrh

My Shopping List!

AMOUNT I HAVE TO SPEND

$ _____

NAME	GIFT	AMOUNT

TOTAL $ _____

Snowman Story

Elf Wheel

Cut out and assemble this "Elf Wheel" with a brass fastener. Cut out the two rectangles, as shown.

Add your own math problems and answers to the wheel on the next page. Move the candy cane to reveal the answer.

cut out

cut out

Make one for each child in class. They will love learning their multiplication tables with "Mr. Elf."

Snowman Math

Start the holiday season with this clever math idea.

Cut several snowmen from white paper. Label each one with a different math problem. Tape the snowmen to popsicle sticks and write the answers on the bottom of the sticks.

7x4   6x3   3x3

* MATH *

Decorate a shallow box with holiday wrapping paper. Cut slits with an art knife and insert each stick so that the answer is hidden.

Students solve the math problems then pull the snowmen to check their answers.

Dreaming of Christmas...

Color Page

TEACHERS: Add your own math problems to Santa. Children can color the picture when work is completed.

December Awards

Name _____

REALLY DID GREAT
IN SCHOOL TODAY!

Date _____

Name _____
was a perfect Santa's
helper today!

Date _____

Name _____

was a wonderful
student today!

Date _____

Teacher _____

Name _____

WAS A REAL JOY
IN CLASS TODAY!

Date _____

Award Ornaments

for a job well done!

Name

Congratulations

Name

GOOD WORK AWARD

Decorate the classroom Christmas tree with these "Award Ornaments."

Copy the ornaments onto colored paper. Students receive an award for each assignment that is completed.

After coloring the ornament, they hang it on the tree.

(Paper clips that have been stretched out make good ornament hangers.)

Super Student Award!

Name

Bookmarks

Ski into the Library for great reading!

"Holidays Around the World"

READ ABOUT IT AT THE LIBRARY

Happy Holidays!

To: From:

BOOKS... a special gift!

Name

Name

Name

Pencil Toppers

Reproduce these "Pencil Toppers" onto construction or index paper. Color and cut out. Use an art knife to cut through the Xs.

Slide a pencil through both Xs as shown.

Give them as student awards or holiday gifts.

Happy Holidays

Hi!

To Ann

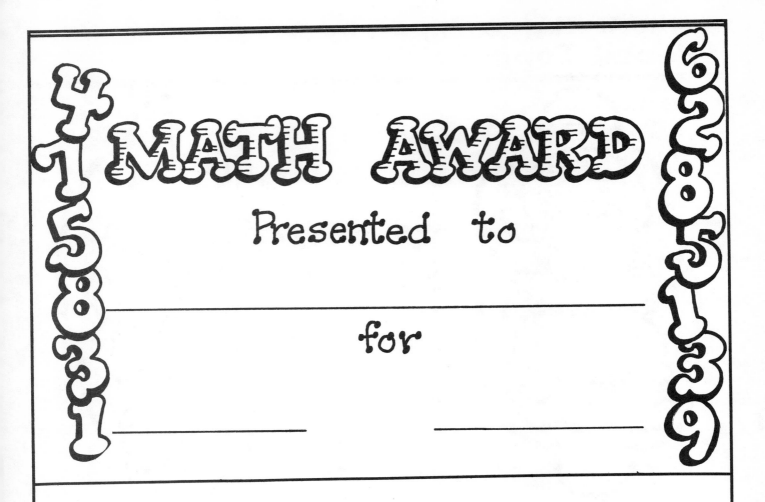

MATH AWARD

Presented to

_____

for

_____   _____

Reading Award

Presented to

_____

for

_____   _____

Good Citizenship Award

Presented to

_____

for

_____   _____

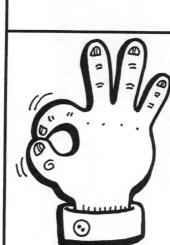

SPELLING AWARD

Presented to

_____

for

_____   _____

Holiday Carolers

Enlarged, these cute carolers can be used in bulletin board displays. You might wish to write holiday greetings on each song book cover. Or, wish visitors to your class a Merry Christmas in several different languages.

As they are, they can be used as gift tags or even bookmarks.

You might even like to make one of them poster board size and attach it to the classroom door. A "Happy Holidays" and your room number would be all you would need.

How ever you choose to use them, you'll find them to bring a very festive spirit to any classroom.

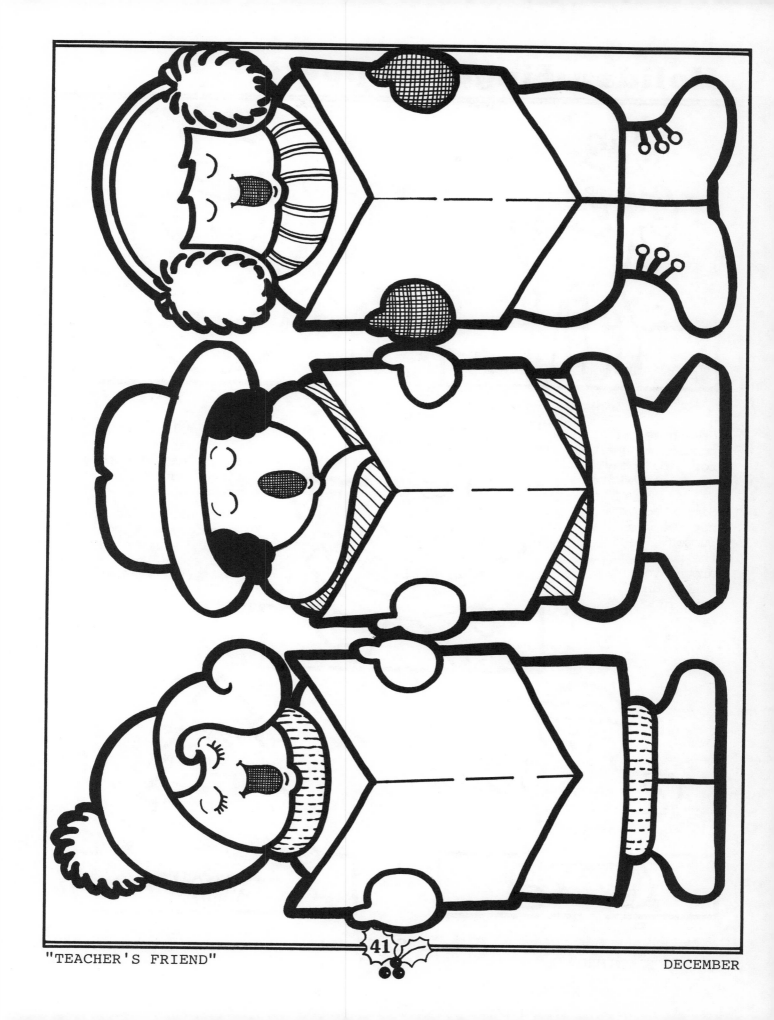

Holiday Finger Puppets

Use these cute finger puppets as awards for good behavior or completed work.

Simply color and cut out each puppet. Bend the puppet around your finger and tape in place.

Students will be eager to do creative writing assignments with these finger puppets as motivators.

Ask each child to choose a puppet and write a story about it. Students can act out their stories in front of the class.

Holiday Crafts

Wreath and Sleigh

Children will love to take this holly wreath home and hang it on the front door!

Cut the center from a paper plate. The outside rim will be the base for the wreath.

Carefully cut holly leaves from green paper. Overlap the leaves as you glue them to the rim. Glue red berries in bunches of three to the wreath. Add a real ribbon bow for a final touch.

Sleigh Decoration

This tiny sleigh can be used as a tree decoration or holiday favor.

Cut one section from a cardboard egg carton and trim to shape. Paint it a holiday color and add glitter if you like. Glue two pipe cleaners on the bottom for sleigh runners. Fill with candy and enjoy!

Snow Scene and Reindeer

This holiday craft will be a cherished possession for years to come.

For each Snow Scene you will need the following:

    Baby food jar
    Spray paint
    Florist clay
    Plastic holiday figure/greenery
    Silver glitter
    White glue

Paint the lid of your baby food jar and let dry. Press a piece of florist clay inside the lid and arrange the plastic figure and greenery in the clay. Squeeze a bead of white glue to the inside lip of the lid.

Fill the jar with water and add about a teaspoon of silver glitter. Carefully place your scene inside the jar, sealing the lid tightly. Let dry overnight in the upside down position. In the morning, shake the snow scene and watch "glittery" snow float down.

Reindeer Door Decoration

Instead of traditional door wreaths, have your students make these charming paper bag reindeer.

Using a large folded grocery bag, tape the bottom corners as shown. Attach yarn to two jingle bells and tape in place, also. Children can use crayons or paper scraps to add features. Cut ears and antlers from brown construction paper and tape to the back of the bag. Have children add their own holiday greeting.

A smaller version can be made using a small lunch sack instead of the large grocery bag.

Stand Up Santa

Cut out and fold this Santa on the dotted lines. Tape the sides together to form a pyramid shape. Hang by a thread as a tree decoration or stand on a table as a mini center piece.

Angel Ornament

Color and cut out the angel pattern. Bend the angel face forward and bring the ends of her dress together in back. Staple the ends together. For a special touch, add cotton or angel hair to the wings and glitter to her dress. Attach a string to the top of her halo to hang from the tree.

Movable Reindeer

Front legs

Back legs

Cut this reindeer pattern from brown construction paper and assemble using brass paper fasteners.

Movable Santa

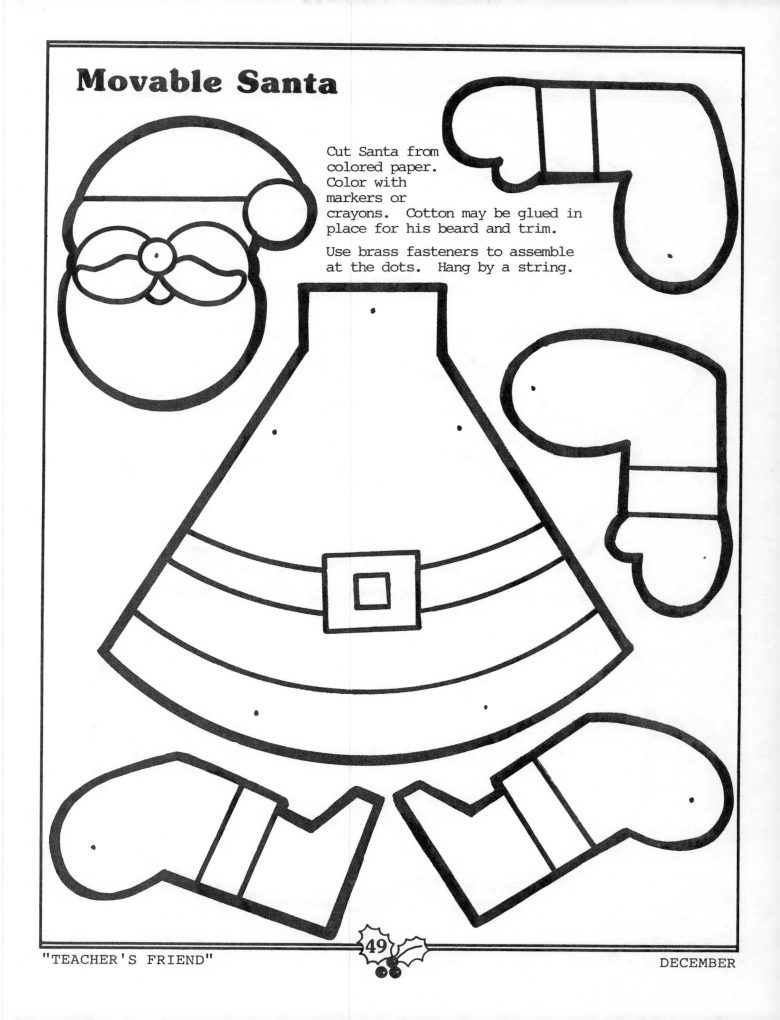

Cut Santa from colored paper. Color with markers or crayons. Cotton may be glued in place for his beard and trim.

Use brass fasteners to assemble at the dots. Hang by a string.

Santa Claus Puppet

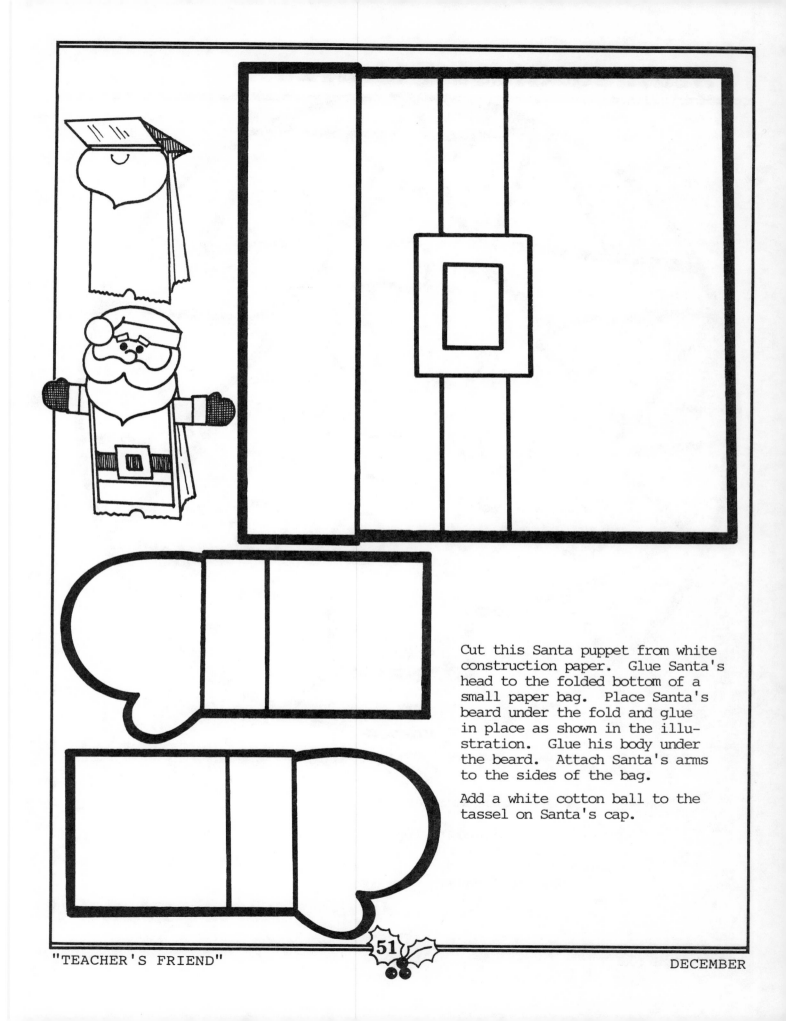

Cut this Santa puppet from white
construction paper. Glue Santa's
head to the folded bottom of a
small paper bag. Place Santa's
beard under the fold and glue
in place as shown in the illustration. Glue his body under
the beard. Attach Santa's arms
to the sides of the bag.

Add a white cotton ball to the
tassel on Santa's cap.

Stained Glass Pictures

These "Stained Glass Pictures" are strikingly beautiful and wonderfully simple to make!

You will need the following materials:

    Permanent colored markers (red, green, yellow and black)
    Plastic food-storage wrap
    Aluminum foil
    Black construction paper
    Tape
    8" paper plates or cardboard circles

Stained Glass Pictures

Tape the patterns to a smooth desk top. Ask each child to stretch a piece of plastic wrap over the pattern of their choice and tape in place. The child colors the picture using the red, green and yellow markers. When the picture is completed, ask the student to trace all of the black lines using the black marker.

The next step is to have the student take a square of foil, measuring one foot, and crumple it carefully. He or she then spreads the foil over a paper plate, taping it in place. Now, the student takes his finished stained glass picture and tapes it over the foil. Mount the entire project on black construction paper and hang in a window or display on the class bulletin board.

Christmas Tree Puppet

Cut colorful paper dots using a hole puncher. Children can decorate their paper bag tree puppet by gluing them in place.

Reindeer Antlers

Children will be delighted to wear these cute "Reindeer Antlers."

Trace the antlers onto brown construction paper and cut out. Make a paper headband for each student and staple the antlers to the sides, as shown.

Snowman Card

Santa Card

Christmas Countdown

Have each child cut out twenty-five small holiday shapes from colored paper. Staple or tie the shapes together in a long string. Remove one shape each day as a countdown to Christmas.

You might like to print the date on each shape.

International Christmas Tree

Wish everyone a Merry Christmas with this "International Christmas Tree." Simply enlarge the tree to bulletin board size. Write holiday greetings in different languages on each ornament.

Feliz Navidad

Gud Jul

Zalig Kerstfeest

Sarbatori Vesele

Froehliche Weihnachten

Noel

Boze Norodzenie

Guon Natale

Hristos Razdajetsia

Nodlaig Mhaith Chugnat

Glaedelig Jul

Hauskaa Joulua

Happy Christmas

Hartlijke Kerstroeten

Shen Tan Kuai Loh

Boas Festas

Customs and Traditions

First Christmas Tree

On Christmas Eve in Germany in 1605, a man by the name of Martin Luther was inspired by the overwhelming beauty of the night sky. It seemed that the heavenly stars appeared to float down and rest on the branches of a wonderful fir tree. Luther wanted to share this magical moment with his family so he cut down the small tree and took it home. There he decorated it with lighted candles. His family rejoiced as they gathered around the first Christmas tree.

Through the years, this custom has spread world wide. The Christmas tree has become a most special holiday tradition with its festive colored lights and shiny glass balls. Even a tiny tree that has few decorations will always symbolize the love that first Christmas tree did so long ago.

(Your students may like to plant a fir tree on the school grounds or perhaps donate a living Christmas tree to a needy family.)

Christmas Gifts

Ever since the Three Wise Men placed their treasures before the Christ Child in Bethlehem, Christmas has been a time of giving gifts.

Through the years, countries around the world have created their own legends and customs of giving gifts at Christmas. In England, Father Christmas brings gifts to family members. In Holland, it's Sinterklaas and in Italy it is La Befana.

Today, this wonderful tradition of giving still touches our hearts in a special way. It is not very difficult to look beyond all the colorful ribbons and bright paper to feel the same spirit of giving as on that very first Christmas. After all, the most precious gift is the gift of love!

(Ask the children to write about a special gift they would like to give someone that money can not buy, a gift of love!)

Customs and Traditions

Christmas Tinsel

Decorating the Christmas tree with shimmering tinsel is an age old tradition. According to legend, a poor old woman was unable to provide decorations for her children's Christmas tree. But when she awoke on Christmas morning, she discovered that a spider had spun a magical silver web which covered the tree. Everyone who saw it was marveled by its glimmering beauty.

Today a touch of tinsel creates a magical quality all its own. Like shimmering jewels these silver strands brighten our hearts during the holiday season.

(After finding a spider web early in the morning, spray it gently with a small amount of white spray paint. Carefully lift the web off using a sheet of black construction paper. The web will adhere to the paper. Collect several and display them on the class bulletin board.)

Mistletoe

Mistletoe is a plant of ancient legends. The Greeks once believed that its evergreen leaves were a symbol of good luck. As years went by, the English ceremoniously cut the mistletoe that grew high in the trees and carried it home in large bundles. During the winter months, they hung it over their doors as a sign of good luck. Since only happiness could pass beneath the mistletoe, enemies would embrace and seal their peace with a kiss of friendship. This is probably where the custom today originated that anyone caught beneath the mistletoe must be kissed.

(Bring some mistletoe to class to show your students. Please explain to them that the mistletoe berries are very poisonous and should never be put in the mouth.)

Customs and Traditions

Green, White & Red

The brilliant colors of green, red and white are our traditional Christmas colors. We use them to decorate our home during the holidays and wrap our packages and gifts.

Legend tells us of a little lamb making his journey to Bethlehem to see the Christ Child. On his way, his snowy white fleece becomes caught on a thorny holly bush. In his struggle to get free, his skin is pricked and tiny droplets of blood freeze as red berries to the branches.

But most people believe the colors come from the richness of the evergreens, the snowy whiteness of the fields in winter, and the red crimson berries of the holly plant. Like many other qualities of Christmas, these merry colors brighten our mood during this hustle bustle time of year.

(Ask children to draw a picture of a Christmas tree and decorate it with thier own chosen holiday colors.)

Christmas Cards

In the year 1870, an Englishman by the name of J.C. Horsely designed a picture on a simple card with a holiday greeting and sent it to his friends. This was the very first Christmas card. Gradually, most everyone sent Christmas cards. Many were very fancy with real lace trim and edges embossed with silver and gold. Today it is still a popular tradition to send cards to faraway family and friends. What a wonderful way to wish people the joys of the holiday season!

(Have the children in your class make special Christmas cards that can be given to patients at a nearby nursing home or hospital. They might like to deliver the cards in person.)

International Greetings

Learn to say "Merry Christmas" in another language!

BELGIUM	Zalig Kerstfeest	FRANCE	Joyeux Noel
CHINA	Shen Tan Kuai Loh	ENGLAND	Happy Christmas
SWEDEN	Gud Jul	GERMANY	Froehliche Weihnachten
RUSSIA	Hristos Razdajetsja	MEXICO	Feliz Navidad
DENMARK	Glaedelig Jul	ITALY	Guon Natale
PORTUGAL	Boas Festas	NETHERLANDS	Hartlijke Kerstroeten
POLAND	Boze Narodzenie	RUMANIA	Sarbatori Vesele
FINLAND	Hauskaa Joulua	IRELAND	Nodlaig Mhaith Chugnat

FIND THE NAMES OF ALL THE COUNTRIES IN THE PUZZLE BELOW.

```
K F T H P O R T U G A L U Y G F I N L A N D A
I V C X O R T M S W F T G B V C X D S F R T I
T D V B L D R U S S I A D R R U M A N I A X R
A D E R A H G T W A S D F G H J U K L I U Y E
L F V G N S E T E F G H Y U C H I N A V C X L
Y W Q A D X S W D E D C V F R T G B N H Y J A
D C V B N H Y H E H Y J U F I L O P M N H U N
L M K J H N Y U N E T H E R L A N D S E V T D
A S C X Z D R F O G Y H H A K T I U R F B H N
G E R M A N Y Y R G Y H J N H I N A T H Y U K
S C V E D T Y T X Y U J I C Y U J K L M N J G
D E R X R T Y H Z R T G Y E D E N M A R K U Y
D F G I G T H T Y H U J K L O I L M J R E S C
Z C B C S E N G L A N D F R T H N M K L O P O
X C Z O J U H N B G T V D C F F B E L G I U M
F G H B V C D R T Y U I P O L M X S W Q E R T
```

ACTIVITY 3

"Peace on Earth"

One way of celebrating the holidays is to emphasize world peace. Post a large white dove on the class bulletin board. Have each student pick a country to study and make a booklet about their Christmas customs. Booklets can be arranged on the board with the word "peace" written in the language of the country they have chosen. A few examples are as follows:

Japan	Heiwa	Italy	Pace
Russia	Mir	Greece	Iri'ni
Isreal	Shalom	Holland	Vrede
Poland	Pokoj	Spain	Paz

What a "peaceful" way to welcome in the holidays and the new year!

Dove of Peace

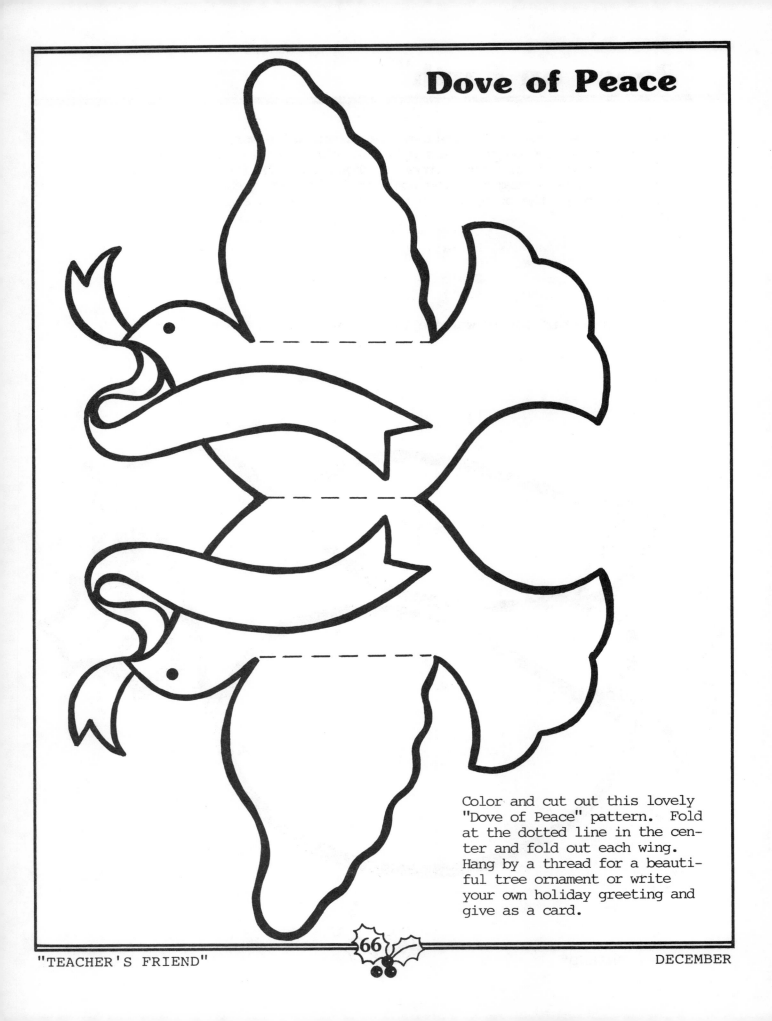

Color and cut out this lovely "Dove of Peace" pattern. Fold at the dotted line in the center and fold out each wing. Hang by a thread for a beautiful tree ornament or write your own holiday greeting and give as a card.

Christmas in Mexico

"Los Posadas"

Christmas in Mexico

In Mexico, the most cherished custom of Christmas is the Posadas. Posadas, meaning lodging, is the name given to the nine days of celebration before "La Navidad," Christmas Day. This celebration commemorates the journey of Mary and Joseph to Bethlehem and their search for lodging each night.

In the country, children gather at private homes. Each child is provided with a candle which is lit as the children form a line and slowly begin to parade down the streets. At the head of this procession two children carry small figures of the Holy Family. As they approach each house they are turned away until they come to a home with the replica of the stable in Bethlehem. There they arrange the figures, placing the Christ Child in the manger, just at midnight.

After prayers before the crèche, there is merrymaking and the breaking of the piñata. Children scramble for the gifts and candy that spill from inside. Fireworks are then set off in celebration.

The children of Mexico receive their gifts on January 6 instead of Christmas Day. This day is known as "Day of the Wise Men." Instead of hanging up their stockings, the children put their shoes out for the Wise Men to fill with toys.

Miniature Piñata

MAKE A MINIATURE PIÑATA AS A CHRISTMAS TREE DECORATION!

You will need:

    styrofoam egg cartons
    felt pens or paint
    yarn
    tissue paper
    glue and scissors
    wrapped candy pieces

Cut an egg cup from your carton and trim the edges. Decorate as you wish. Push a piece of yarn through the top for hanging. Cut two strips of tissue paper, 3" X 6". Clip the bottom edge to make a fringe. Glue the top of the strips to the inside edge of your cup. Fasten a wrapped piece of candy to the inside of the piñata with tape.

There you have it! A perfect miniature piñata to hang on the tree or give as a gift!

Feliz Navidad Word Find

FIND THESE WORDS ASSOCIATED WITH CHRISTMAS IN MEXICO.

CHRISTMAS, MEXICO, PIÑATA, POSADAS, NAVIDAD, JOSEPH, MARY, CHRIST CHILD, BETHLEHEM, STABLE

```
N D F G H Y C H R I S T M A S G Y U I O P H J K
A S D F G T Y U I K L O P M J K U I L O J M K L
V S D F G H M A R Y B H U K I O L P J H Y U I P
I S D F R T G H Y U J K I L O P M N O G T Y H N
D F G T H Y U J K I O M N V B N H Y S E R T Y U
A S D B E T H L E H E M G T Y U J H E S W E R T
D F G T Y G H U I K O P K L K I O M P F R T M A
S D F R T Y H U J K I O L M N B V D H F R T E R
P O S A D A S D R T Y U I O K J H B N M H U X D
Z X C F R T Y G B V F C D S W A X C G H J U I G
A S D F R T G Y H C H R I S T C H I L D H U C S
A X C F R T S T A B L E F T Y U H J K I N K O L
A X Z C V B H U J K L M N B V C X Z S E R T Y U
A X D R T Y H B N J I K L O P M N B G T R F V X
Z X S D C V F G B N H J U J K I P I N A T A W E
R T Y U H G F D S W Q A X C V B N J K L O F D T
```

ACTIVITY 4

"FELIZ NAVIDAD"

Celebrate "Feliz Navidad" with this festive bulletin board.

Cut a large bird or animal shape from stiff poster board for the piñata. Cover with pieces of colorful tissue paper squares and streamers. Pin it to the board with the heading "Feliz Navidad!" Post students' stories about "Los Posadas" around the piñata.

You might like to save the piñata for future use during Cinco de Mayo or Mexico Independence Day.

"TEACHER'S FRIEND"

International Children - Mexico

Creative Writing

Christmas in Italy

Christmas in Italy

Several days before Christmas, the children of Italy go door to door singing favorite Christmas carols. They are often accompanied by pipers wearing bright red jackets and broad-brimmed hats with red tassels. They carry bagpipes, flutes and oboes, on which they play sweet holiday music. Often the children and pipers are invited into homes to sing old carols and folk songs.

On Christmas Eve, many candles are lit as the children in the family take turns telling the wonderful story of Christmas and the birth of the holy "Bambino." At this time, Italian families gather around their beloved "Presepio," a shrine to the Holy Child, and pray. After a 24-hour fast, all members of the family then sit down to a feast of delicious lasagna and spaghetti.

On the twelfth day of the holidays, January 6, a kindly old witch known as "La Befana" brings gifts to the children. Legend has it that when Christ was born, the shepherds told La Befana of the wondrous happenings and the guiding star, but she delayed setting out. Every Christmas since, she wanders in search of the Holy Child, leaving gifts at each home in hope of finding Him inside.

La Befana is often shown as being old and ugly, but the children of Italy love her very much. That is unless they have been naughty, for then their shoes will be filled with coal and ashes instead of candy and gifts.

EASY MINI PIZZAS

In celebration of Christmas in Italy have each child make their own mini pizza!

Give each student one half of an English muffin. Spoon 1 tablespoon prepared pizza sauce on top and add grated cheese. Pepperoni or sliced olives can also be added. Bake in a conventional or microwave oven until the cheese bubbles.

Children will love having this little taste of Italy during the holidays!

"La Befana"

PASTE HERE

PASTE HERE

La Befana

Ask students to color and cut out "La Befana."

Cut strips of paper 4½" X 12". Have children write their thoughts about Christmas in Italy on the strips.

Accordian fold each strip and glue both ends in place.

Attach a string to the top of her hat and hang in the class-room.

International Children - Italy

International Children - Italy

Creative Writing

Christmas in Holland

Sinterklaas Day

Christmas in Holland

During the last weekend in November, "Sinterklaas," (Santa Clause) arrives in Holland on a large steamboat from his home in Spain. Along with him he brings his white horse and dozens of his helpers, "Zwarte Piets," (Black Peters.) They accompany Sinterklaas to Amsterdam, where large crowds come out to greet him in person.

Before Sinterklaas Day, December 6, small children try to be very good. If they are naughty, Zwarte Piet may swat them with a birch stick or worse yet, take them away to Spain in his big bag. During this time, adults and older children are busy preparing surprise gifts for the family. The presents are wrapped in funny, unusual ways with special notes written in verse. The gifts are then hidden away until Sinterklaas Day.

The night before Sinterklaas Day, children place their wooden shoes by the fireplace, filled with carrots or hay for the white horse. In the morning, they hope these things will be replaced with gifts from Sinterklaas. In some homes, the doorbell rings and Piet's hand will throw candies and cookies into the room, quickly slamming the door behind. Children run to gather the sweets while mother pulls in a large basket of gifts left outside. In other homes, gifts are not opened until little children have gone to bed. Then the rest of the family will open presents and read the attached poems signed by "Sinterklaas."

A traditional holiday sweet is marzipan, which is an almond paste candy shaped into funny things such as animals or fruit. Initials of pure chocolate are also a favorite.

As you can see, Sinterklaas Day is a very happy time with festive celebrations and much merrymaking. Christmas Day, however, is celebrated in a very quiet way with family get-togethers and church services.

WRITE THESE WORDS ON THE CLASS-
ROOM CHALK BOARD AND ASK STUDENTS
TO WRITE THEIR OWN STORIES ABOUT
"SINTERKLAAS."

Holland
Sinterklaas
Zwarte Piet
Steamboat
Spain
White Horse
Wooden Shoe
Gifts

Poems from Sinterklaas

On Sinterklaas Day, December 6th, families have a great deal of fun playing tricks on one another.

You might create a classroom treasure hunt where one clue leads to other clues hidden all over the classroom. The "treasure," (a bag of cookies or other treats) should be hidden in a clever place at the end of the search.

As a creative writing activity have students write funny poems to each other as they do in Holland. Have children draw names so that no one is left out. Each poem should be addressed to an individual child and signed by "Sinterklaas!" (Remember to emphasize that only "nice" poems will be accepted.)

Children can take turns reading their "Sinterklaas notes" to the rest of the class.

To: Cindy

She's the best speller. She really is good!

If only she'd spell the words should, would and could!

Sinterklaas

To: Jimmy

He often stays up late on Saturday night.

Getting out of bed Sunday takes all of his might!

Sinterklaas

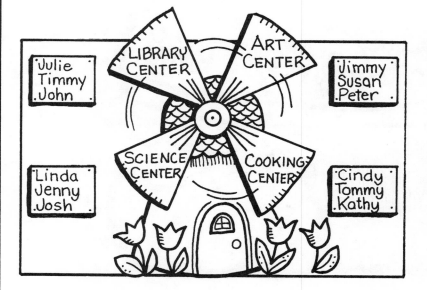

"DUTCH TREAT"

Create a real "Dutch Treat" in the classroom with this special windmill.

Mount the paper windmill onto the class bulletin board. Cut the blades from heavy poster board and attach it in the center with straight pins. The windmill blades should be turned periodically to direct children to particular center activities.

International Children - Holland

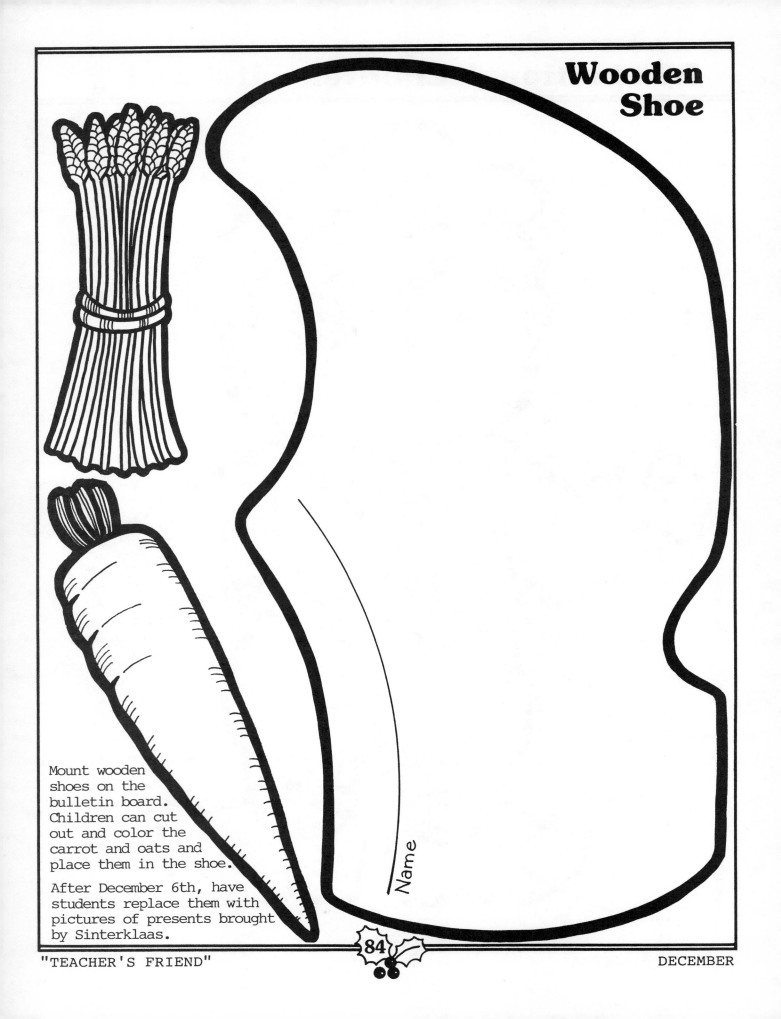

Wooden Shoe

Mount wooden shoes on the bulletin board. Children can cut out and color the carrot and oats and place them in the shoe.

After December 6th, have students replace them with pictures of presents brought by Sinterklaas.

Name

Windmill

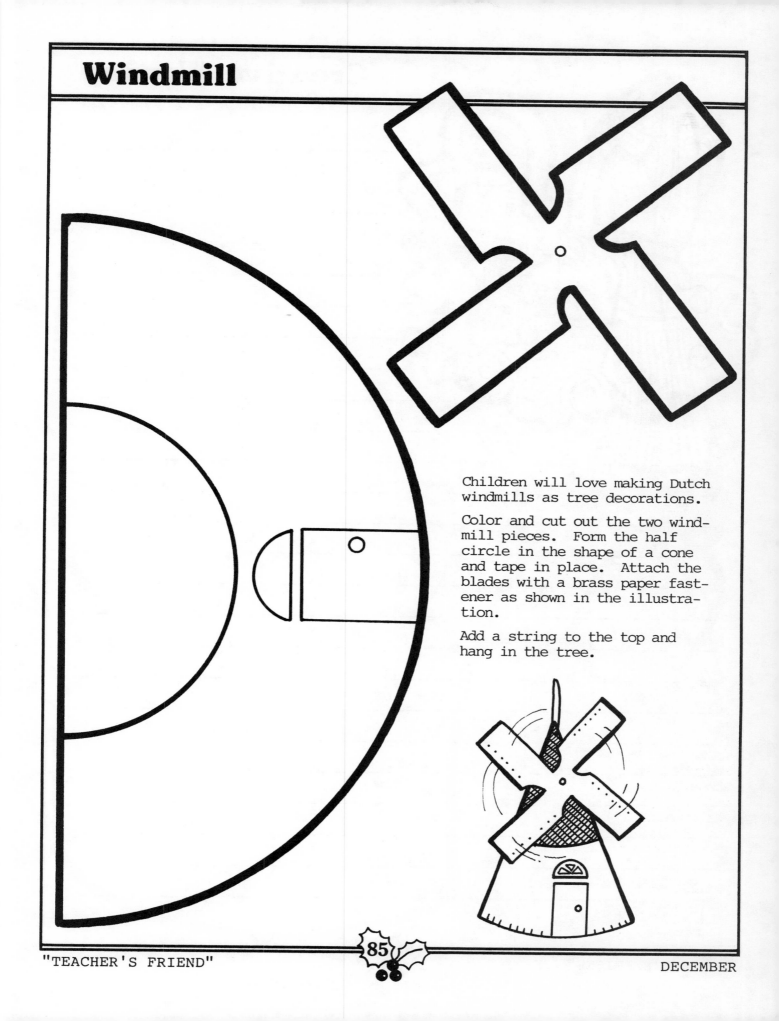

Children will love making Dutch windmills as tree decorations.

Color and cut out the two windmill pieces. Form the half circle in the shape of a cone and tape in place. Attach the blades with a brass paper fastener as shown in the illustration.

Add a string to the top and hang in the tree.

Creative Writing

Christmas in Sweden

Santa Lucia Day

Christmas in Sweden

On December 13, one of the shortest days of the year, the feast of Santa Lucia is celebrated in Sweden. Dressed in a white gown and wearing a wreath of lighted candles on her head, the eldest daughter in each family, representing Santa Lucia, brings good will and light to the long winter's night. Early in the morning, she prepares sweet cakes and coffee for each member of the family while they are still in bed. She then wakens the family by singing the old song "Santa Lucia."

On Christmas Eve, the houses are prepared for "Jultomten," Father Christmas, who arrives in a sleigh assisted by miniatures of himself. The tree is decorated with real lighted candles. At midnight, the story of the first Christmas is read aloud and gifts are opened. Christmas Day itself is very quiet, with church services early in the morning and the rest of the day spent at home with the entire family.

Santa Lucia

Santa Lucia was a young girl that lived in Italy in the second century A.D. She was a very strong believer in the Christian religion, which was banned in her country at the time. Lucia thought that her family should give all of their wealth to the poor, but family members strongly disagreed with her.

One day her mother became very ill. Lucia persuaded her to make a journey to a Christian holy place. Lucia's mother was cured and in gratitude for this miracle agreed to give away her wealth. Several days later the government discovered that Lucia was a Christian and put her to death. Centuries later, in honor of her good deeds, Lucia was declared a saint by the church. The name Lucia means light, so she became the saint of vision and light.

Although this story is several hundred years old, Santa Lucia Day was observed in only a few Swedish villages until recently. There it was believed that Santa Lucia could be seen on her special day serving hot rolls and drink to the poor people.

Santa Lucia Day falls on one of the shortest days in the year, December 13. In Sweden, the winter nights are so long that in the far north the sun only shines for about one hour. What could be more cheerful than to honor Santa Lucia with this festival of light and goodwill.

Santa Lucia Sweet Rolls

SANTA LUCIA SWEET ROLLS

Ingredients: 5 cups of Bisquick
2 eggs
6 tablespoons cooking oil
3/4 cup milk

Combine the ingredients in the order given.
Divide the dough so that each child has a
piece. Ask the children to shape the dough
into 8" long rolls and curl the ends to form
an "S" shape, as shown. Add raisins for decoration if you wish. Bake on a greased
cookie sheet at 375 degrees for about 15 min-
utes.

While they are baking, prepare a frosting
made with 1½ cups powdered sugar and 5 tea-
spoons milk. While the rolls are still warm
from the oven, brush with the frosting.

"OUR BRIGHT LIGHTS"

This "bright" bulletin board
idea will tie in nicely with
your studies of Santa Lucia.

Cut one candle and flame from
construction paper for each
child in class. Arrange on
the bulletin board as shown.
(Holly or other leaves across
the bottom add a nice touch.)

Award gold stars or stickers
for all completed assignments.
The children will love to
place them on their own candles for classmates to see.

Santa Lucia Headwreaths

Every girl in class can become Santa Lucia for a day with this headwreath pattern.

Cut paper headbands for every girl. Students can cut their own candles from yellow or white construction paper. Leaves can be cut from green paper. Fasten the candles and leaves to the headbands with glue or staples.

Fit the headwreath to the students's head and staple in place.

The girls may like to pass out cook-ies to the boys as they sing the old song, "Santa Lucia."

Hanukkah

"Festival of Lights"

Hanukkah

Hanukkah is a happy midwinter festival celebrated by the Jewish people. The holiday is honored for eight days beginning on the twenty-fifth day of the Hebrew month of Kislev falling within the months of November or December. Hanukkah commemorates the victory of the Maccabbes over the Syrians in 165 B.C.

The Jews of Palestine, under the leadership of Judas Maccabeus, successfully fought a war against King Antiochus. The King had forced all of his subjects to practice the religion of Greece. Jews were denied their religious freedom. During this time, Palestine was under Syrian-Greek rule. When the Maccabbes returned to their temple previously occupied by the Greeks, they found only enough sacred oil to light the holy menorah for one day. By divine miracle, however, the lamp continued to burn for eight days. In celebration, the event was called the "Festival of Lights."

Today, Jewish families celebrate this event by lighting a special candelabra called a menorah. The holiday begins the first day by lighting the first candle at sundown on the twenty-fourth of Kislev. A "servant" candle called Shammash is also lighted each night and is used to light the other candles. Each evening an additional candle is burned until all eight candles are burning together. At this time, family members say blessings of thanks to God.

After lighting the Menorah, games are played and gifts exchanged by the family. Children especially like the holiday of Hanukkah. The ancient game using a four sided top known as the dreydl is played and traditional holiday goodies such as "latkes," potato pancakes are served. The custom of gift giving is also very special and has been included in Hanukkah celebrations for centuries.

The Dreydl

A dreydl is a special four sided top. The Hebrew letters <u>N</u>, <u>G</u>, <u>H</u>, and <u>S</u> are written on the sides of the top. These letters stand for the words <u>Nes</u>, <u>Gadol</u>, <u>Haya</u> and <u>Sham</u>, which mean "a great miracle happened." Long ago, Jewish people were forbidden to come together and pray. In order to practice their religion they pretended to play games with this little top. Here is how to play a game with the dreydl.

Assemble the dreydl pattern on page 100 according to the directions. Give ten dried beans to each player and place an empty bowl in the center of the table. Before each turn, every player must put a bean in the bowl. The players take turns spinning the top. If the letter "N" turns up the player wins no beans; if "G" turns up he wins all the beans in the bowl; if "H" turns up he wins half the beans in the bowl and if "S" turns up he must put one bean in the bowl. The game continues until one player has won all the beans.

Hanukkah Word Find

ACTIVITY 5

```
B N M K J H A N U K K A H C B G F D T Y J K
J W R T Y U I O P K L J M N B G F D S F G Y
E W D F T G H Y T H Y U J S E R T X Z A I T
W S F R D R E Y D L S E M S E R F V X F F W
I E R D S C I G T H Y Y E D F C Y U I O T Q
S W E R T R G S E Y U I N D Q A T Y U O S M
H H A S E F H B V C S B O W X N U I O P L J
K J H G D E T W X V J K R N M D E Y U O P L
M A C C A B B E S L R T A R G L G H J U K I
A S D F R T Y H G F V B H J T E U I O P L N
A S W Q E L A T K E S F R E R S K L I G H T
X Z C V B N H Y T G F R E D S W Q M K L O P
S H A M M A S H Y B V F R E D C X S Y H K L
S E R T H J K I U Y N J P R A Y E R S G N M
W X C V G Y T R F B H U J K O P L M H Y T B
S E R F V D C T H F E S T I V A L R F G H J
S D F R T Y H J U I K L O P M B G T F V C D
A F A M I L Y E R F V G Y U J N H G B V D E
```

FIND THESE HANUKKAH WORDS: MACCABBES, DREYDL, JEWISH, MENORAH, HANUKKAH, EIGHT, CANDLES, GIFTS, LATKES, FESTIVAL, LIGHT, FAMILY, SHAMMASH, PRAYERS

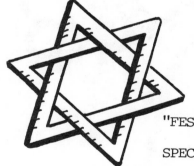

MATCH THESE FACTS ABOUT HANUKKAH

"FESTIVAL OF LIGHTS"   DREYDL

SPECIAL JEWISH CANDELABRA   MENORAH

THE NUMBER OF CANDLES   HANUKKAH

THE "SERVANT" CANDLE   JUDAS MACCABEUS

FOUR SIDED TOP GAME   LATKES

LEADER OF THE MACCABBES   SHAMMASH

POTATO PANCAKES   EIGHT

ACTIVITY 6

International Children - Israel

Star of David

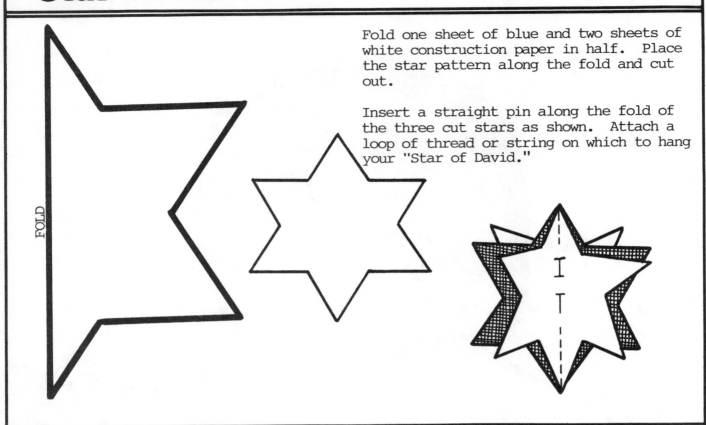

FOLD

Fold one sheet of blue and two sheets of white construction paper in half. Place the star pattern along the fold and cut out.

Insert a straight pin along the fold of the three cut stars as shown. Attach a loop of thread or string on which to hang your "Star of David."

"HAPPY HANUKKAH"

Create a festive Hanukkah bulletin board with this simple idea.

Use patterns cut in shapes of Hanukkah symbols. Have students trace the shapes on construction paper. Ask them to write interesting facts or creative stories about this special Jewish holiday.

Mount the title "Happy Hanukkah" and display the new creations.

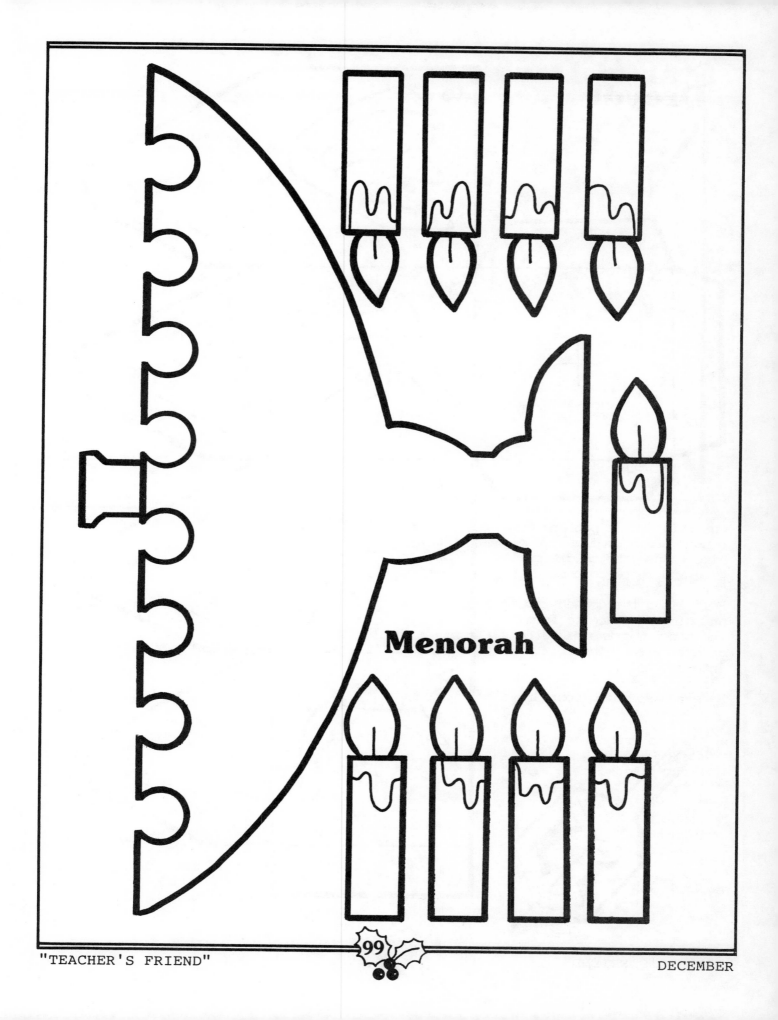

Menorah

Dreydl

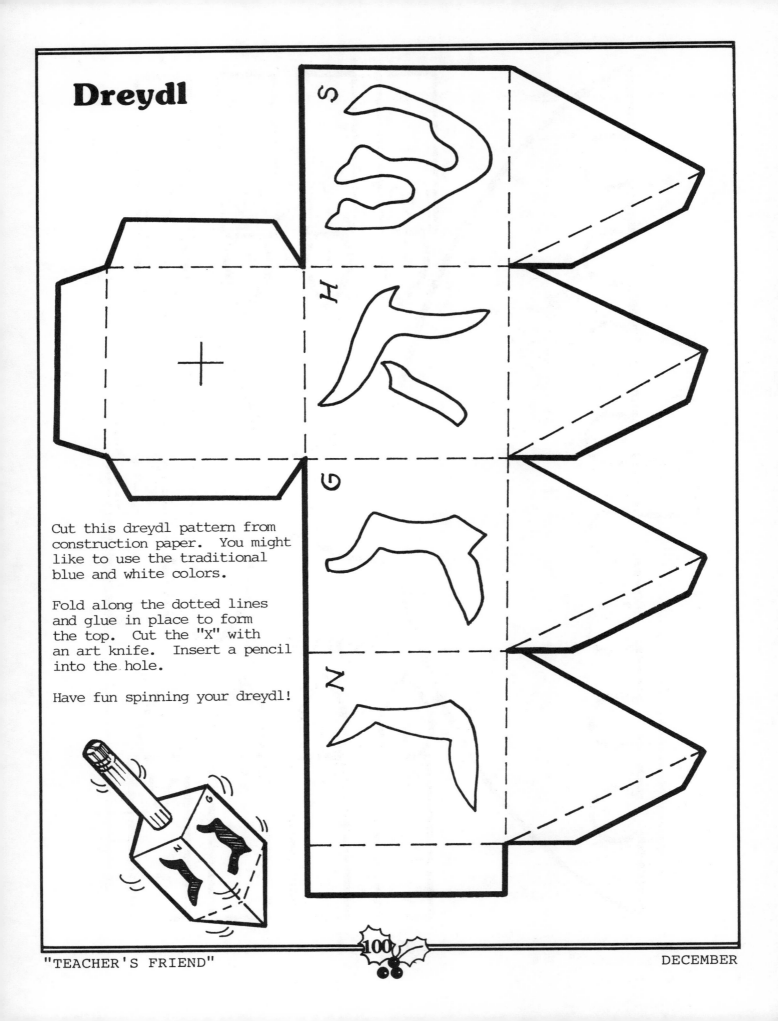

Cut this dreydl pattern from construction paper. You might like to use the traditional blue and white colors.

Fold along the dotted lines and glue in place to form the top. Cut the "X" with an art knife. Insert a pencil into the hole.

Have fun spinning your dreydl!

December's Best!

Bulletin Boards

PEACE ON EARTH

Mount a large map of the world on the class bulletin board or draw your own. Cut berries and holly leaves from construction paper and pin them to form a wreath around the map. Students can write papers about their solutions to the world problems.

HANDSOME CHRISTMAS TREE

Ask each student to trace and cut two handprints from green construction paper. Have them write their name in bold letters in the center of each handprint. Curl the fingers with a pencil. Pin the handprints to the class bulletin board as illustrated. This is a "handsome" way to make a class Christmas tree.

If you end up with too many handprints, make a wreath for the classroom door, also.

GIFT OF LOVE

A "Gift of Love" is one which money cannot buy.

Ask children to design holiday packages using real wrapping paper and ribbon. Each student is to write a paper about a "gift of love" they would like to give and display it on the board under their package. Visitors can flip up a corner of the package to read the paper.

and more...

CANDY CANE NAME DISPLAY

Children will love to see their names displayed on this cheery bulletin board.

Cut a large candy cane from poster board or butcher paper. Use red paint or markers to add the red stripes. Children can sign their own names or you can do it for them. Large paper holly can announce your holiday greeting.

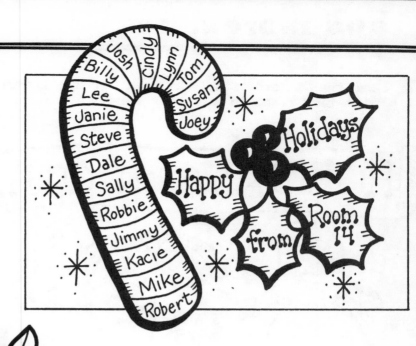

12 DAYS TILL CHRISTMAS VACATION

Green foil leaves and yellow paper pears make this clever holiday bulletin board.

Arrange the leaves and pears on a large paper cut tree pattern. Write the numbers one to twelve on the pears. Remove one pear each day as a count down to Christmas vacation.

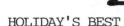

HOLIDAY'S BEST

Make these festive candles by displaying good work papers on 9" X 12" red construction paper. Attach a bright yellow paper flame to the top of each candle. Add the title "Holiday's Best" to the top of the board. Attach paper holly as decoration to this easy to make bulletin board display.

and more...

Use the "International Children" in this book for a bulletin board idea that ties right in with your seasonal studies. Add a title and student's research papers to complete the board.

HOLIDAYS IN OTHER LANDS

To make this warm and cozy fireplace cut red construction paper into 6" X 9" rectangles. Pin the rectangles to the class bulletin board as shown in the illustration to make the bricks. Cut one long strip of paper for the mantel and label with the teacher's name and grade. Write a student's name on each stocking and pin to the mantel. Fill the stockings with take-home awards. Let the children take the stockings home the last day before vacation.

MRS. PETER'S ~ 4TH GRADE

Tammy   Jamie   Carol   Bret   Paul

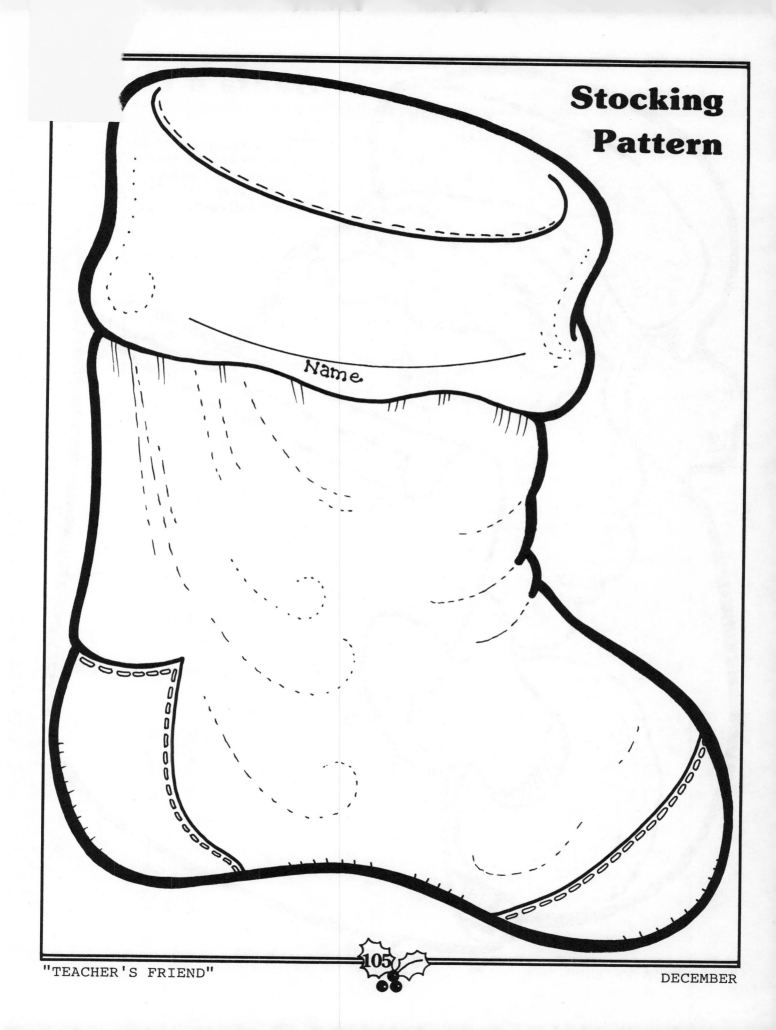

Name

Santa's List

Create a great holiday bulletin board by enlarging this cute Santa. Children can write their own names on Santa's list as a welcome to classroom visitors.

Partridge and Pear Tree

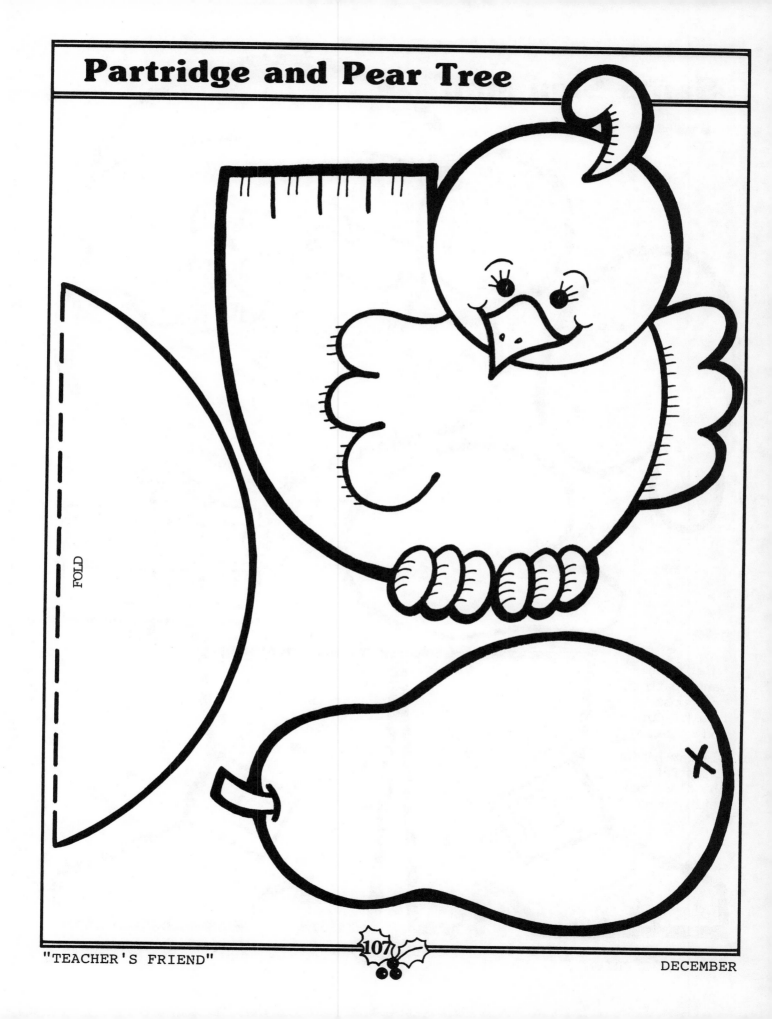

FOLD

Santa Sign Man

Enlarge this Santa pattern onto posterboard. Cut out and color.

Display him as illustrated on the class bulletin board.

French Horn and Angel

Enlarged, these patterns can announce coming events or proclaim good classroom work.

Answer Key

ACTIVITY 1

UNSCRAMBLE SANTA'S REINDEER NAMES.

Z N E T I L B	BLITZEN
P D I U C	CUPID
X I N V E	VIXEN
H S R E A D	DASHER
M O T E C	COMET
C A N D R E	DANCER
D U L O H P R	RUDOLPH
C R N E A R P	PRANCER
D D N O R E	DONDER

ACTIVITY 2

CAN YOU FIND ALL OF THE DECORATIONS FOR THE TREE?

CANDYCANES, ORNAMENTS, ANGEL, TINSEL, STAR, BOWS, BELLS, GARLAND, ICICLES, LIGHTS and PINECONES

```
L K I J H O P L L L M N B V C S T A R H N J K O P
W C V G H J B O W S S D F G Y T R E D F V B N M K
S D R T G F H R Y N J H U I K D E R T I G T Y H J
G G T Y H J U N R E W Q R T Y U I K L C D R T Y U
A D E R T H C A N D Y C A N E S K L J I D F T F G
R F T Y J G H M N B Y N A L R U D R T C F G Y U M
L F G T H Y N E J K R E W X Z A N G E L M J G Y R
A D E R T Y H N D F B C F R T Y H J H E G H N M K
N F T F T G H T I N S E L B H J U I L S D R T S X
D F G T H Y U S K I L O J E F T G H U J N B V C X
P I N E C O N E S T Y H N L G Y U I P R E W D S F
B G H U Y T F G H J U I K L G V B N M K L P O I U
S E R T H J U I O K J M N S E D C V B N M K J U Y
S E R T G F V B H J K L I G H T S E W R T F G H J
A S D C V B N M K J H G F D S A T R E W Y U I O P
R F D E S W Q A Z X C V B H G Y T U I J K L O P U
```

ACTIVITY 3

```
K F T H P O R T U G A L U Y G F I N L A N D A
I V C X O R T M S W F T G B V C X D S F R T I
T D V B L D R U S S I A D R R U M A N I A X R
A D E R A H G T W A S D F G H J U K L I U Y E
L F V G N S E T E F G H Y U C H I N A V C X L
Y W Q A D X S W D E D C V F R T G B N H Y J A
D C V B N H Y H E H Y J U F I L O P M N H U N
L M K J H N Y U N E T H E R L A N D S E V T D
A S C X Z D R F O G Y H H A K T I U R F B H N
G E R M A N Y Y R G Y H J N H I N A T H Y U K
S C V E D T Y T X Y U J I C Y U J K L M N J G
D E R X R T Y H Z R T G Y E D E N M A R K U Y
D F G I G T H T Y H U J K L O I L M J R E S C
Z C B C S E N G L A N D F R T H N M K L O P O
X C Z O J U H N B G T V D C F F B E L G I U M
F G H B V C D R T Y U I P O L M X S W Q E R T
```

Answer Key

ACTIVITY 4

FIND THESE WORDS ASSOCIATED WITH CHRISTMAS IN MEXICO.

CHRISTMAS, MEXICO, PINATA, POSADAS, NAVIDAD, JOSEPH, MARY, CHRIST CHILD, BETHLEHEM, STABLE

```
N D F G H Y C H R I S T M A S G Y U I O P H J K
A S D F G T Y U I K L O P M J K U I L O J M K L
V S D F G H M A R Y B H U K I O L P J H Y U I P
I S D F R T G H Y U J K I L O P M N O G T Y H N
D F G T H Y U J K I Q M N V B N H Y S E R T Y U
A S D B E T H L E H E M G T Y U J H E S W E R T
D F G T Y G H U I K O P K L K I O M P F R T M A
S D F R T Y H U J K I O L M N B V D H F R T E R
P O S A D A S D R T Y U I O K J H B N M H U X D
Z X C F R T Y G B V F C D S W A X C G H J U I G
A S D F R T G Y H C H R I S T C H I L D H U C S
A X C F R T S T A B L E F T Y U H J K I N K O L
A X Z C V B H U J K L M N B V C X Z S E R T Y U
A X D R T Y H B N J I K L O P M N B G T R F V X
Z X S D C V F G B N H J U J K I P I N A T A W E
R T Y U H G F D S W Q A X C V B N J K L O F D T
```

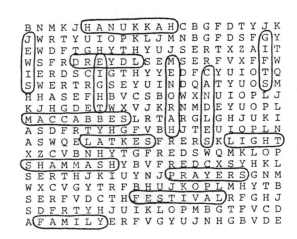

ACTIVITY 5

```
B N M K J H A N U K K A H C B G F D T Y J K
J W R T Y U I O P K L J M N B G F D S F G Y
E W D F T G H Y T H Y U J S E R T X Z A I T
W S F R D R E Y D L S E M S E R F V X F F W
I E R D S C I G T H Y Y E D F C Y U I O T Q
S W E R T R G S E Y U I N D Q A T Y U O S M
H H A S E F H B V C S B O W X N U I O P L J
K J H G D E T W X V J K R N M D E Y U O P L
M A C C A B B E S L R T A R G L G H J U K I
A S D F R T Y H G F V B H J T E U I O P L N
A S W Q E L A T K E S F R E R S K L I G H T
X Z C V B N H Y T G F R E D S W Q M K L O P
S H A M M A S H Y B V F R E D C X S Y H K L
S E R T H J K I U Y N J P R A Y E R S G N M
W X C V G Y T R F B H U J K O P L M H Y T B
S E R F V D C T H F E S T I V A L R F G H J
S D F R T Y H J U I K L O P M B G T F V C D
A F A M I L Y E R F V G Y U J N H G B V D E
```

ACTIVITY 6

MATCH THESE FACTS ABOUT HANUKKAH

"FESTIVAL OF LIGHTS"   DREYDL

SPECIAL JEWISH CANDELABRA   MENORAH

THE NUMBER OF CANDLES   HANUKKAH

THE "SERVANT" CANDLE   JUDAS MACCABEUS

FOUR SIDED TOP GAME   LATKES

LEADER OF THE MACCABBES   SHAMMASH

POTATO PANCAKES   EIGHT